Bulgaria

by Meish Goldish

Consultant: Marjorie Faulstich Orellana, PhD
Professor of Urban Schooling
University of California, Los Angeles

BEARPORT
PUBLISHING

New York, New York

Credits

Cover, © Get4Net/Dreamstime and © S-F/Shutterstock; TOC, © Anna Chelnokova/Shutterstock; 4, © Todoranko/Shutterstock; 5T, © Mitzo/Shutterstock; 5B, © Konrad Wothe/imageBROKER/Alamy; 7, © Nenov/iStock; 8, © KpaTyH/Shutterstock; 9T, © stoyanh/Shutterstock; 9B, © Impact Press Group/ZUMA Press/Newscom; 10, © Ron van Elst/Shutterstock; 11T, © Mirko Graul/Shutterstock; 11B, © Ondrej Prosicky/Shutterstock; 12L, © meunierd/Shutterstock; 12–13, © Lmspencer/Shutterstock; 14, © eivanov/Shutterstock; 15, © NurPhoto/Alamy; 16, © Anton Chalakov/Shutterstock; 17T, © Circlephoto/Shutterstock; 17BL, © RaDoll/Shutterstock; 17BR, © szefei/Shutterstock; 18, © Anneka/Shutterstock; 19, © Jan Csernoch/Alamy; 20, © NoirChocolate/Shutterstock; 21T, © NataLogPhoto/Shutterstock; 21B, © nikolay100/Shutterstock; 22, © Marholev/iStock; 23, © Ilko Iliev/Alamy; 24T, © Stoyan Nenov/Reuters/Newscom; 24B, © Chavdar Stoychev/Shutterstock; 25, © Msgagov/Dreamstime; 26, © Pencho Tihov/Alamy; 27T, © Nataliya Nazarova/Shutterstock; 27B, © Ewa Rejmer/Alamy; 28, © Lukas Gojda/Shutterstock; 29T, © mikimad/iStock; 29B, © Yiannis Kourtoglou/Reuters/Newscom; 30T, © Ivan Vdovin/Alamy and © Alex-505/Shutterstock; 30B, © Nicks Stock Store/Shutterstock; 31 (T to B), © royaltystockphoto/Shutterstock, © Mileatanasov/Dreamstime, © Nataliya Nazarova/Shutterstock, © ntonkova/Shutterstock, and © S. Kat/Shutterstock; 32, © rook76/Shutterstock.

Publisher: Kenn Goin
Senior Editor: Joyce Tavolacci
Creative Director: Spencer Brinker
Design: Debrah Kaiser
Photo Researcher: Thomas Persano

Library of Congress Cataloging-in-Publication Data

Names: Goldish, Meish, author.
Title: Bulgaria / by Meish Goldish.
Description: New York, New York : Bearport Publishing, 2020. | Series:
  Countries we come from | Includes bibliographical references and index. |
  Audience: Ages 6–12.
Identifiers: LCCN 2019007200 (print) | LCCN 2019009261 (ebook) | ISBN
  9781642805901 (ebook) | ISBN 9781642805369 (library)
Subjects: LCSH: Bulgaria—Juvenile literature.
Classification: LCC DR67.7 (ebook) | LCC DR67.7 .G64 2020 (print) | DDC
  949.9—dc23
LC record available at https://lccn.loc.gov/2019007200

For more information, write to Bearport Publishing Company, Inc., 45 West 21st Street, Suite 3B, New York, New York 10010. Printed in the United States of America.

10 9 8 7 6 5 4 3 2 1

Contents

This Is Bulgaria

Colorful

ANCIENT

Happy

Bulgaria is a country in southeastern Europe.

It sits on the Black Sea.

The country is about the same size as Tennessee.

a beach on
the Black Sea

Bulgaria is home
to over seven
million people.

Mountains rise high in Bulgaria.

In between the mountains is rich farmland.

Dense forests cover about one-third of the land.

a sunflower farm

Bulgaria has over 700 **hot springs**—more than any other European country! People relax in the warm waters.

9

Bulgaria is home to amazing animals!

Brown bears and wolves roam the mountains.

Hedgehogs live in the forests and villages.

They help people by eating dangerous snakes.

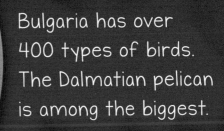

Dalmatian pelicans

Bulgaria has over 400 types of birds. The Dalmatian pelican is among the biggest.

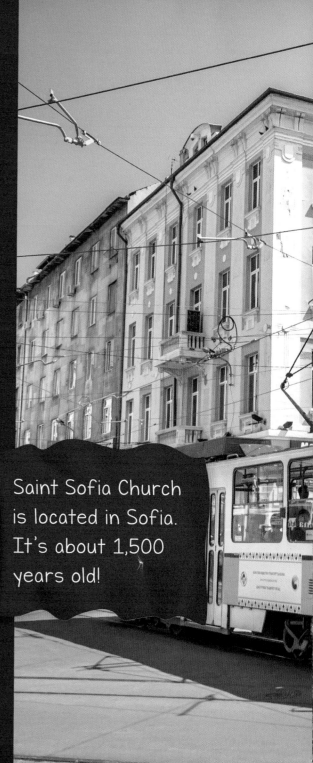

Most Bulgarians live in cities.

Bulgaria's biggest city and **capital** is Sofia.

Over one million people live there.

Saint Sofia Church is located in Sofia. It's about 1,500 years old!

People have lived in Bulgaria for thousands of years.

Over time, different groups have ruled the land.

an ancient Roman building in Bulgaria

Turkey controlled Bulgaria for about 500 years, until 1878.

In 1908, Bulgaria became a free country.

In the 1400s, Turkey fought Poland to control Bulgaria. Today, Bulgarians remember their past by acting out the old battles.

Bulgarians have many kinds of jobs.

A lot of people work in factories.

They make fabrics, cars, and other things.

Other people work in hospitals, hotels, and restaurants.

Some Bulgarians collect rose petals. The petals are used to make perfume!

In Bulgaria, most people speak Bulgarian.

This is how you say *good morning* in Bulgarian:

Dobro utro
(DOH-broh OO-troh)

This is how you say *good evening*:

Dobar vecher
(DOH-bur
VETCH-uhr)

Bulgarians nod up and down to mean "no." They shake their head from side to side to mean "yes!"

What's for dinner?

shopska salad

Bulgarians love to eat *shopska* (SHOP-skuh) salad.

It has tomatoes, cucumbers, onions, peppers, and cheese.

Banitsa (BAN-eet-sah) is a flaky pastry filled with cheese.
Yum!

banitsa

Bulgarian yogurt has a special taste. It's made with **bacteria** found in no other country!

What else is interesting about Bulgaria?

The country has unusual rocks!

Some are named for things they look like.

Squirrel rock

The Belogradchik Fortress was built in between these strange rocks.

The Belogradchik Fortress is 2,000 years old! The giant rocks helped to keep out enemies.

23

Bulgaria has buried treasure!

In 1972, gold items were discovered in the city of Varna.

The gold came from ancient Thracian (THREY-shuhn) **tombs**.

Most of the tombs have yet to be explored.

inside a Thracian tomb

The Thracians were an ancient tribe. They lived in Bulgaria about 5,000 to 7,000 years ago.

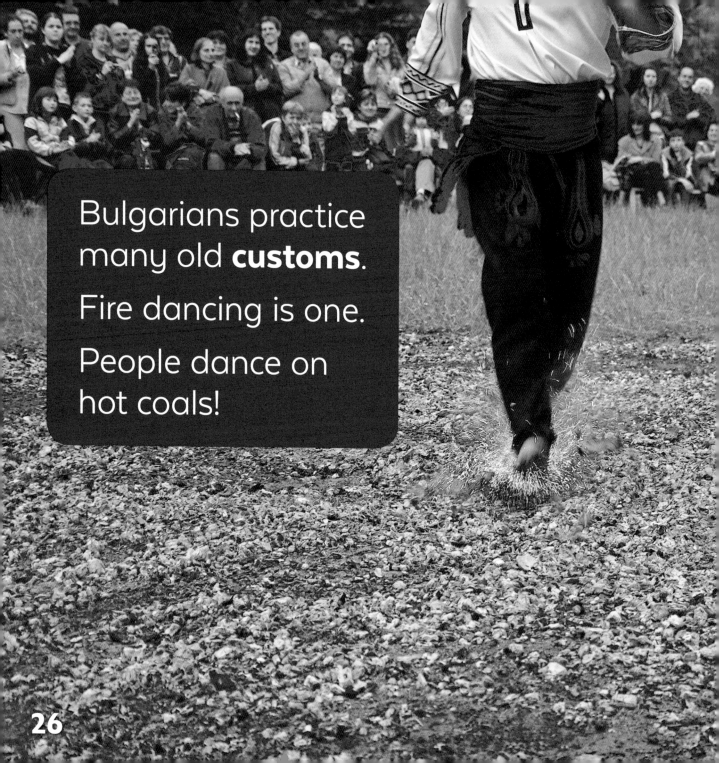

Bulgarians practice many old **customs**.

Fire dancing is one.

People dance on hot coals!

On March 1, Bulgarians welcome spring.

They give each other *martenitsas* (mahr-tuh-NEET-suhs) for health and happiness.

martenitsas

Martenitsas are made of red and white string. People wear them as bracelets or hang them on trees.

What's a favorite
sport in Bulgaria?

Skiing!

Other popular sports are basketball and volleyball.

Bulgarians also love soccer.

Go team, go!

In Bulgaria, soccer is called football.

Fast Facts

Capital city: Sofia

Population of Bulgaria: Over seven million

Main language: Bulgarian

Money: Bulgarian lev

Major religion: Christianity

Neighboring countries include: Greece, Macedonia, Romania, Serbia, and Turkey

Cool Fact: A recording of a Bulgarian folk song has been traveling on a spacecraft since 1977!

bacteria (bak-TIHR-ee-uh) tiny living things, some of which are used in the making of foods

capital (KAP-uh-tuhl) the city where a country's government is based

customs (KUSS-tuhmz) the usual ways of doing things

hot springs (HOT SPRINGZ) places where naturally hot water rises to Earth's surface

tombs (TOOMZ) graves, rooms, or buildings for holding dead bodies

Index

Read More

Goldstein, Margaret J. *Bulgaria in Pictures (Visual Geography Series).* Minneapolis, MN: Lerner (2005).

Mattern, Joanne. *Bulgaria (Cultures of the World).* New York: Cavendish Square (2017).

Learn More Online

To learn more about Bulgaria, visit
www.bearportpublishing.com/CountriesWeComeFrom

About the Author

Meish Goldish lives in New York.
He has written more than 300 books for children.